Success As A Self-Development Authority

By: Justin Bickham

SUCCESS AS A SELF-DEVELOPMENT AUTHORITY 1

TABLE OF CONTENTS

CHAPTER 1 -- INTRODUCTION

Do you have the passion or ambition to help others? Are you diligent in your own pursuit of Self-Development? Have you transformed your life and now want to teach others your secret? If you answered yes to any of these questions, then a career as a Self-Development authority could be your calling.

Throughout history people have searched for ways to improve themselves, whether financially, physically, personally, spiritually, or a combination thereof. As human beings, we want to better ourselves; it is our nature. We want to improve ourselves, achieve more, reach our goals, and raise the bar. It's only natural that we are competitive.

Since the beginning of time, ambitious people have attributed some indescribable secret to success. People have spent thousands of dollars and many hours trying to cultivate these secrets, and they will continue to do so. Particularly since the early 1970s, there has been a growing trend for people attending classes, workshops, and seminars that will enable them to align their thinking and their actions with those who have achieved success. They continue to do so to this day.

Therefore, there is a continually growing demand for Self-Development professionals to this day, especially during these volatile times. Unemployment is higher than usual, and those who have been laid off from and are out of work for an unusually long period of time have lost or are starting to lose confidence in the ways of the world. This is the reason for the growing demand for the Self-Development industry as there are people out there who wish to regain their confidence and motivation to achieve success.

Although many will not admit it, deep down, people do have the desire to succeed. Most of the time it just takes that extra little push to get them going. This is where the Self-Development profession comes in to play.

CHAPTER 2 -- WHAT IS SELF-DEVELOPMENT?

If you want to get into the Self-Development profession, you have to know what Self-Development is, right?

Self-Development is a concept that improves awareness and identity, develops talent and potential, builds character, improves the quality of life, and helps one to realize individual goals and dreams. It is more complex than self-help. Self-Development is also about taking personal responsibility for one's life and actions through observation and assessment and using that to better one's self.

In addition, Self-Development is also about developing other individuals, whether as a teacher, spiritual leader, or a motivational speaker. This is why I decided to write this guide. If you have improved your well-being after learning from a Self-Development Authority, whether that Authority being a teacher, spiritual leader, or motivational speaker, you may be inspired to share what you have learned with others who may be seeking guidance. It's knowledge that must be passed along; it doesn't stop at one person. This is why you may want to consider a career as a Self-Development Authority. But before you do, you must ask yourself, *is the Self-Development industry right for you?*

CHAPTER 3 -- IS THE SELF-DEVELOPMENT INDUSTRY RIGHT FOR YOU?

Getting into the Self-Development industry isn't difficult. First and foremost, you need the knowledge and ability to teach others. Over the years you have most likely acquired knowledge and methods from many other authorities. From that knowledge and those methods, it's highly probable that you have developed you own ideas that you can share with others. Establishing a clear purpose is essential. Your focus should represent your strengths as well as your abilities. If you are a natural at public speaking, then consider something along the lines of a motivational speaker. There is a high demand for people who enjoy public speaking. Being a motivational speaker embraces giving people confidence to reach their potential. If you have a unique style to present your Self-Development methods verbally, then develop that skill.

The popularity of best-selling how-to books such as *Winning Is Believing, Think And Grow Rich, How To Develop A Winning Personality, Overcoming Shyness, Imagineering, New Life Options, Winning By Negotiation, Successful Visual-Verbal Communications, Conversationally Speaking,* and countless other books lend reinforcement to the "need" for Self-Development seminars.

You can promote and stage these seminars either as a generalist or as a specialist in a specific area of expertise--and make money for yourself in this lesser known but highly demanding field! The Self-Development market potential has only barely scratched the surface, thus affording a real ground-floor opportunity for those with the initiative to take action.

Dale Carnegie--author of *How To Win Friends and Influence People*--was certainly one of the first, if not "the first" Self-Development authority. During the Great Depression, he recognized the need for people to improve themselves. Carnegie worked out a deal with the management of his local YMCA, spread the word of his classes on Self-Development, and the rest is one of the truly classic unemployed-to-multi-million-dollar success stories of our time.

A Self-Development seminar is conducted much the same as a Toastmaster's Club meeting. It can be held anywhere, from an informal setting such as someone's living room to as formal as a Convention Center.

Basically, a Self-Development seminar is a gathering where one or more speakers speak on a specific subject. More often than not, only a certain aspect of Self-Development, such as *How to Develop a Positive/Mental Attitude*--is the main topic of the seminar. In other words, the more successful seminars deal with "specialized areas" of Self-Development.

Self-Development seminars usually wrap up with audience participation through question and answer sessions. Many "wind down" with the speaker circulating through the audience; there is also an opportunity to purchase books, audios, and videos created by the speakers and other Self-Development authorities that provide on-going motivation and reinforcement to what was talked about at the seminar. Always, maybe even as the featured subject of the seminar, a great deal of motivation and inspiration is projected during these meetings. The bottom line is, motivation is the main purpose of Self-Development seminars more so than the attendees learning something they don't already know. The favorite words of most seminar speakers is usually, "It's the difference between having a dream and taking action--a matter of saying ‘I can’, believing it, and then doing it--because you can!

This is why successful seminars are generally based upon the concept of giving you the power to believe you can. The speaker usually speaks from insights and expertise gained from his/her own life experiences. Self-Development seminars give the attendees the tools and the motivation to succeed. Thus, a well-organized and well-presented seminar that helps people climb the ladder of success can't help but succeed because we are a success oriented society. It's an easy sell with an income potential limited only by your ability to express yourself.

So do you think the Self-Development industry is right for you? If you are still reading it might very well could be. If you are a firm believer in yourself and you can conduct a meeting, then you are already ahead of the game, but if you're still not sure if this industry is right for you, keep reading on to the next chapter and learn about some of the benefits and schematics of this highly rewarding industry.

CHAPTER 4 -- BENEFITS AND SCHEMATICS OF THE SELF-DEVELOPMENT INDUSTRY

There are benefits you can obtain from being involved in the rewarding Self-Development industry. We are going to go over some of these benefits here. We will also go over some of the schematics of what this industry entails.

What's great about this industry is you don't need an office to make it big in the Self-Development industry. The public doesn't visit you; you take your programs to them. Self-Development seminars appeal to almost everybody—from blue-collar workers to top executives. People pay on average about $300 to attend a Self-Development seminar, so your basic audience will probably come from the upper-income brackets, but if you can promote your seminar in a certain way, that is, to promote according to your target audience, you can pull in attendees from other income brackets as well.

Many people promoting these seminars use sales teams to call upon top company executives to either get them to pay part of the cost for several employees to attend these seminars as educational or work development investments or to foot the bill to sponsor a "group seminar" for that company's middle management. You will find these types of seminars in Convention Centers or even hotel meeting rooms, depending on the size of the audience. Personnel from different companies will be in attendance of these specialty-type seminars, which provides not only educational and motivational experiences, but also networking opportunities for these individuals, not to mention referrals for future seminars. With specialty-type seminars, such as those for career development, many specialty speakers can make in excess of $200,000 per year with these type of motivational and/or Self-Development seminars.

However you will probably start out small by staging seminars for the general public in your church's Fellowship Hall, restaurant banquet rooms, hotel meeting rooms, and community centers. This will entail advertising costs, costs for renting the space, and costs for copies of material you will hand out to attendees. There will also be costs for additional material you may want to sell to attendees.

Generally, you might want to try radio advertising during the week before your seminar date. So you should invest in that as well as in the local newspapers. For newspaper advertisings you should start placing picture ads about a month before the seminar date. Some seminar promoters invest about a quarter of their budget in newspapers with some of that going into radio advertising. Of course, the allocation of your advertising budget should be related to the previous proven pulling power of each media within that particular market. A lot of television advertising is done with guest appearances on local talk and news shows.

Of course social media is a great inexpensive way to promote Self-Development seminars. Sites like Facebook, Twitter, Pintrest, Meetup, and LinkedIn are great for promoting these seminars. With social media, you can connect with companies who may be interested in sending their employees to these seminars. You can create a Facebook page with information on your upcoming seminars including pictures of previous seminars as well as testimonials from people who have attended any of your seminars in the past. If this is your first seminar, talk about what you wish to accomplish and what you hope attendees would get out of your seminar. Talk about the benefits and how they can develop themselves by attending your seminar. You would also include a webpage on your Twitter and LinkedIn pages so people can click on to register for your seminar.

By being a guest on a local talk or news show, you can give those watching a taste of what is to come at your seminar, maybe a sample of what is to come. You can also do this through social media by posting a video on your Facebook, Twitter, and LinkedIn pages. Speaking of which, YouTube is another social media site you can use to promote your upcoming Self-Development seminar. You can make a short video giving a sample of what is to come at your seminar, just something brief that you can make as if you were conducting the seminar. Also, if you're a guest on a talk or news show, you might want to ask for a copy of the video from your guest appearance, but the video will probably show up on that talk or news show's website, so you'll have promotion for that as well.

If you so choose, you could conduct your seminar for free. Free seminars tend to draw huge crowds, during which special "front people" turn everybody on with super-motivational stories designed to wet the appetite of those in attendance for more. These free seminars are generally brief and may strictly be motivational in purpose, but you may want to do a whole seminar for free. In this case you can make money from the sale of transcripts from the seminar or an audio or a video recording of the seminar. There's also an opportunity to sell audio and video recordings of previous seminars, books, etc. This is also a great opportunity to offer attendees a chance to sign up on a mailing or email list where you can promote upcoming seminars, new audio recordings, and any new material you come up with.

At the end of a free seminar, you can pass out brochures describing any upcoming events, or products relating to this seminar, or any past or future seminars. You can also send out newsletters to those who have signed up on your email list. These newsletters can include articles relating to the Self-Development industry as well as information on upcoming products and events, not to mention current products for sale. With good promoting and attractive newsletters, you can count on closing about 30 to 35% of those who attend your free seminars.

There are two options you can take to make money from holding seminars. You can set a large price for attending the seminar, or you can charge a smaller price, or even offer the seminar for free. In the latter case, you can sell a written transcript of the seminar, an audio recording, or even a video of the seminar. You can also sell transcripts, recordings, or videos from previous seminars. If people who attend sign up on an email list, in addition to advertising for future seminars in your e-newsletters, you can also promote material from these future seminars or products you may have created between seminars.

Attendees can use these materials as a reference if they want to recall what they have learned from the seminar.

These are some of the benefits and schematics of the Self-Development industry. You can see that this is a rewarding opportunity, and it does involve being outgoing and getting up and speaking in front of large crowds. But what if you don't feel comfortable speaking in from of large groups or if you feel shy? You can still make money in the Self-Development industry. The next chapter talks about Self-Development opportunities outside of conducting seminars.

CHAPTER 5 -- SELF-DEVELOPMENT OPPORTUNITES OUTSIDE OF SEMINARS

If you don't feel comfortable being the principal speaker at your seminars, you can hire local sales training people, professional people from the medical specialties or any specialty related to the topic of your seminar, local "experts" known through your area newspapers or broadcast media, people you know through social media, or nationally known speakers willing to travel who operate through speakers' bureaus. You can find a list by searching on Google for speakers' bureaus. What you might want to do is contact these places and see about getting an estimate for them having someone coming to speak at your seminars.

Maybe you feel more comfortable with the written word. If so you can start an online Self-Development business. Creating a website is easier than ever and is relatively inexpensive. Most website hosting and design companies are more than eager to have your business. They compete to offer packages to ensure the success of your website. Once you have outlined your initial goals for your website, maintaining and keeping your site current is easy. All you need is a positive attitude and the ability to provide valuable service. I cannot stress the importance of value enough. The content on your site should be top notch. There are way too many websites out there that do nothing but lead you elsewhere. Some websites have nothing but affiliate links and not enough informative content. That's why you should research other Self-Development websites and determine what works for you.

If you want to inspire people but feel shy about the prospect of going it alone, then opt for those Self-Development entrepreneur businesses already operating. Many have franchises or training programs. Some can teach you the business end of operations, while others may groom you to be a life coach. Always research the company that you are interested in. There are good, legitimate companies available that you can get involved with. On the flip side, there are also scams and empty promises running rampant in the cyber world. Seek out companies with solid reputations.

So whether you start your own Self-Development business website or purchase an existing business, you can make money by creating and selling your own Self-Development products, whether they are books/e-books, audio, or video recordings. If you wish you can also use your business to promote products from Amazon and Clickbank as an affiliate, but make sure you provide valuable content to your visitors because no one wants to see a website with a bunch of affiliate links. Also, be sure to offer your visitors an opportunity to sign up for an e-newsletter so they can keep up to date on what you are doing in your business as well as receive motivational tips from you.

The Self-Development entrepreneur business arena is flourishing. There is always room for more of these businesses because people crave new information. New approaches are always needed, and they are developing at an increasing rate. The world continues to evolve and change constantly, and individuals also need to do so in order to keep up. Self-Development skills and life strategies restore hope to those who have lost it or wish to gain it for the first time. This is an area that makes people feel good by believing in being successful.

Being a life coach is another opportunity. You may not feel comfortable speaking in front of large crowds, but you might feel more comfortable in a one-to-one setting. As a life coach you are like a counselor. You can motivate and inspire others on an individual basis, and by that you can cater to their individual needs and desires. What you would do is help your clients set and accomplish personal goals. Those goals could be career or personal related, wherever your client desires to change his or her life. Depending on what area your client desires to change, you may be able to help that individual. Life coaches can make up to around $100,000 per year and are Self-Development authorities, so this may be an area you may want to consider.

By beginning your own transformation to a new career, you can take your passion and fly. If you like people and want to make a difference in people's lives, then the Self-Development industry just might be right for you. You might have something special you can offer to others that just may become the next big thing in the Self-Development industry.

To reiterate, there are thousands out there who are looking to improve themselves and are willing to pay someone to inspire them and help them find their way. You can start in the Self-Development business by hosting meetings in your home, a meeting room in a local restaurant or hotel, a community center, or even your church Fellowship hall. All it takes is action on your part to get started, but before you get started, you may want to learn a little more about a Self-Development home based business.

CHAPTER 6 -- A LITTLE MORE ABOUT A SELF-DEVELOPMENT HOME BASED BUSINESS

There really is a need for Self-Development home based businesses. Self-Development is a top priority. In business, employees who improve their skills improve their chances of getting raises and promotions. In relationships, people improve their connections by obtaining better communication skills. On a deeper note, we are all trying to take charge of ourselves and control our destiny. We can no longer be content with just settling for what we have in our lives when we know knowledge is power. Today our collective momentum is born out of the choice to live a conscious lifestyle. Fulfillment can be found in being mindful of the choices we make and the accountability we take towards those choices.

Self-Development home based businesses have been around for many years. However, the Self-Development boom has jumped exponentially since the success of the book and movie *The Secret*. In this popular book "The Laws of Attraction" became a catalyst for getting what you want out of life. It is this ideology that is responsible for this fresh breath of air in the Self-Development industry. *The Secret* is an outspoken reminder to desire all things possible within our lifetime.

So should you consider a Self-Development home based business? If you are passionate about mentoring others, or if you are knowledgeable of Self-Development skills and resources, then this just might be for you. You can choose a specific area to focus on, or you can choose a general area. Whichever you choose, you can focus on your particular strengths which are desired in teaching others. The worse reason you can get into the Self-Development industry is to just make money. Yes, there is a lot of money to be made in this industry, but getting into this industry just to make money is the wrong reason to do so. In fact, it is the absolute wrong reason to get into any high paying industry, or any industry for that matter. If you are in it just for the money, you will not be happy in what you are doing, meaning you would not be successful in whatever industry you are in, meaning you will not be able to provide the quality service people are seeking. There are too many people out there who are seeking genuine help with their life, and it would be a disservice to those who seek that help and the Self-Development industry.

So when you embark on such a career choice, you should evaluate your purpose and what area you will specialize in. Do you hold a special ability to motivate people? Then perhaps being a motivational speaker is for you. You could focus your area around public speaking seminars. Once you identify your purpose in the Self-Development field, you can design a plan for success. If the idea of going at this alone scares you, then consider joining a legitimate Self-Development franchise where you can work from home. Many of these types of organizations are always looking for healthy additions to their business.

The future for growth in the Self-Development fields looks positive. We are increasingly starving for improvement and for complete control of our lives. We all want spiritual enlightenment, physical and emotional well-being, and financial freedom. We are craving to feel complete in our lives. We are living new truths about ourselves, and we are examining our co-existence. Desiring new information, people are actively seeking out Self-Development opportunities. The demand for knowledge on Self-Development is limitless. This field provides those seeking with not only the tools for change, but also the inspiration and the confidence. There is no other field that exists today that can provide any type of positive renewal like Self-Development.

This is what a Self-Development business is all about. It is about having the desire to motivate others to become successful. There is just one more item to discuss that you must know in order to be successful in and be able to provide a fulfilling experience with in the Self-Development industry.

CHAPTER 7 -- SUCCESSFUL PEOPLE...

In order to be successful in the Self-Development industry as well as provide people with a fulfilling experience, you must know what makes people successful. This means you must be successful as well, otherwise, the motivation you provide just doesn't work. People can see right through your mask. This is why you must know what makes people successful, or else you will not be successful in helping others become successful, and then you wouldn't have done your job.

With that, what makes people successful? Below are some traits of successful people. Successful people…

1. Are willing to try new things, knowing that if they don't succeed, failure is often a cleverly disguised learning opportunity.

2. Believe in and trust themselves first and foremost. They don't have to check with

others to make decisions; they instinctively know what is right for them and go after it!

3. Have a well-developed life strategy with a written life vision/mission, purpose, and a statement of goals.

4. Get things done, through whatever organizational/time management system that works for them. They make the most of each day and take action on important life tasks each and every day.

5. Are able to discern (see clearly) other's reasons and motives, so they selectively choose who and what to align themselves with. They surround themselves with only the highest quality people, programs, and places.

6. Tap into the collective brainpower of others by reading books, magazines, and articles---anything that is helpful for their own development.

7. Value the learning process for learning's sake. They do not learn just to get a

certificate, degree, title, etc. They learn because it is fundamentally rewarding for them.

8. Are the teachers of the world, who share their knowledge with other people. They put themselves out there so the rest of us can benefit, and in exchange, they develop and grow their own learning.

9. Do not like to stay the same. They love to grow and develop. They also often reinvent themselves time and time again to stay ahead of the game.

10. Not only know about specific subjects and topics, but also know what it means to be human at this time as we evolve. We as humans are avidly curious and want to know more about becoming bigger and brighter, and as a result we evolve naturally.

So do you have the above traits? If you, the Self-Development industry is definitely right for you. But remember, do not go into this industry unless you want to help and motivate others better themselves all around, and in turn better yourself. In order to be successful you must be open minded and willing to grow yourself. It doesn't help you trying to help others grow if you remain close minded and are not willing to grow yourself. This is why if you're only interested in working in Self-Development for the money being to absolute wrong reason for being in this industry. The absolute right reason for being a Self-Development authority is so you can motivate and enlighten others to become consciously aware of the world around them, while at the same time doing this yourself. All in all your efforts with help all humans evolve and make this world a better place.

So, are you ready? Get out there and change the world!

www.ingramcontent.com/pod-product-compliance
Ingram Content Group UK Ltd.
Pitfield, Milton Keynes, MK11 3LW, UK
UKHW041903190726
13854UKWH00003B/1056